Ardmore, Oklahoma

DK READERS

Level 3

Spacebusters: The Race to the Moon
Beastly Tales
Shark Attack!
Titanic
Invaders from Outer Space
Movie Magic
Plants Bite Back!
Time Traveler
Bermuda Triangle
Tiger Tales
Aladdin
Heidi
Zeppelin: The Age of the Airship
Spies
Terror on the Amazon
Disasters at Sea
The Story of Anne Frank
Abraham Lincoln: Lawyer, Leader, Legend
George Washington: Soldier, Hero, President
Extreme Sports
Spiders' Secrets

The Big Dinosaur Dig
Space Heroes: Amazing Astronauts
The Story of Chocolate
School Days Around the World
Polar Bear Alert!
NFL: Whiz Kid Quarterbacks
MLB: Home Run Heroes: Big Mac, Sammy, and Junior
MLB: World Series Heroes
MLB: Record Breakers
MLB: Down to the Wire: Baseball's Great Pennant Races
Star Wars: Star Pilot
Star Wars: I want to be a Jedi
The X-Men School
Abraham Lincoln: Abogado, Líder, Leyenda en español
Al Espacio: La Carrera a la Luna en español
Fantastic Four: The World's Greatest Superteam
Marvel Heroes: Amazing Powers

Level 4

Days of the Knights
Volcanoes and Other Natural Disasters
Secrets of the Mummies
Pirates! Raiders of the High Seas
Horse Heroes
Trojan Horse
Micro Monsters
Going for Gold!
Extreme Machines
Flying Ace: The Story of Amelia Earhart
Robin Hood
Black Beauty
Free at Last! The Story of Martin Luther King, Jr.
Joan of Arc
Spooky Spinechillers
Welcome to The Globe! The Story of Shakespeare's Theater
Antarctic Adventure
Space Station: Accident on Mir
Atlantis: The Lost City?
Dinosaur Detectives
Danger on the Mountain: Scaling the World's Highest Peaks
Crime Busters
The Story of Muhammad Ali
First Flight: The Story of the Wright Brothers
D-Day Landings: the Story of the Allied Invasion
Solo Sailing
Thomas Edison: The Great Inventor
Dinosaurs! Battle of the Bones
NFL: NFL's Greatest Upsets
NFL: Rumbling Running Backs
NFL: Super Bowl!
MLB: Strikeout Kings

MLB: Super Shortstops: Jeter, Nomar, and A-Rod
MLB: The Story of the New York Yankees
MLB: The World of Baseball
MLB: October Magic: All the Best World Series!
WCW: Feel the Sting
WCW: Going for Goldberg
JLA: Batman's Guide to Crime and Detection
JLA: Superman's Guide to the Universe
JLA: Aquaman's Guide to the Oceans
JLA: Wonder Woman's Book of Myths
JLA: Flash's Guide to Speed
JLA: Green Lantern's Guide to Great Inventions
The Story of the X-Men: How it all Began
Creating the X-Men: How Comic Books Come to Life
Spider-Man's Amazing Powers
The Story of Spider-Man
The Incredible Hulk's Book of Strength
The Story of the Incredible Hulk
Transformers: The Awakening
Transformers: The Quest
Transformers: The Unicron Battles
Transformers: The Uprising
Transformers: Megatron Returns
Transformers: Terracon Attack
Star Wars: Galactic Crisis!
Star Wars: Beware the Dark Side
Star Wars: Epic Battles
Fantastic Four: Evil Adversaries
Marvel Heroes: Greatest Battles

A Note to Parents

DK READERS is a compelling program for beginning readers, designed in conjunction with leading literacy experts, including Dr. Linda Gambrell, Professor of Education at Clemson University. Dr. Gambrell has served as President of the national Reading Conference, the College Reading Association, and the International Reading Association.

Beautiful illustrations and superb full-color photographs combine with engaging, easy-to-read text to offer a fresh approach to each subject in the series. Each DK READER is guaranteed to capture a child's interest while developing his or her reading skills, general knowledge, and love of reading.

The five levels of DK READERS are aimed at different reading abilities, enabling you to choose the books that are exactly right for your child:

Pre-level 1: Learning to read
Level 1: Beginning to read
Level 2: Beginning to read alone
Level 3: Reading alone
Level 4: Proficient readers

The "normal" age at which a child begins to read can be anywhere from three to eight years old, so these levels are only a general guideline.

No matter which level you select, you can be sure that you are helping your child learn to read, then read to learn!

LONDON, NEW YORK, MUNICH,
MELBOURNE, AND DELHI

Senior Editor Catherine Saunders
Designer Sandra Perry
Editorial Assistant Jo Casey
Brand Manager Lisa Lanzarini
Publishing Manager Simon Beecroft
Category Publisher Alex Allan
Production Editor Sean Daly
Production Nick Seston

Reading Consultant
Linda Gambrell

Lucasfilm Ltd.
Executive Editor Jonathan Rinzler
Art Director Troy Alders
Continuity Editor Leland Chee
Director of Publishing Carol Roeder

First published in the United States in 2008 by
DK Publishing
375 Hudson Street
New York, New York 10014

07 08 09 10 11 10 9 8 7 6 5 4 3 2 1
SD349 – 12/07

A catalog record for this book is available from the Library of Congress.

ISBN 978-0-7566-3602-9 (paperback)
ISBN 978-0-7566-3605-0 (hardback)

Color reproduction by GRB Editrice S.r.l., London
Printed and bound by L-Rex, China.

Discover more at
www.dk.com

Contents

The Story of Darth Vader 4
Young Anakin Skywalker 6
A Special Calling 8
A New Life Begins 10
Jedi Training 12
Increasing Frustration 14
Powerful Friend 16
Unstoppable Feelings 18
Turning to the Dark Side 20
Jedi Hero 22
The Dark Side Wins 24
The End of Anakin 26
Rebuilding Darth Vader 28
Padmé's Secret 30
The Rise of Darth Vader 32
Civil War 34
Rebel Victory 36
Imperial Fleet 38
Vader's Revenge 40
Cloud City 42
Vader's Choice 44
The Death of Darth Vader 46
Glossary 48

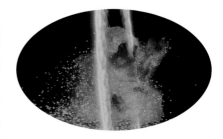

DK READERS

THE STORY OF
DARTH VADER

READING **3** ALONE

Written by Catherine Saunders

The Story of Darth Vader

Take a look at Darth Vader—if you dare! He is a very dangerous man with many terrifying powers. Darth Vader is a ruthless Sith Lord who helps rule the galaxy for the evil Emperor Palpatine.

But Darth Vader was not always the masked Sith you see now. Once he was a talented Jedi Knight named Anakin Skywalker. Read on and uncover the story of how a promising young Jedi turned to the dark side of the Force.

Emperor Palpatine
From the first moment he met Anakin Skywalker, Palpatine knew that he could be the perfect apprentice.

Young Anakin Skywalker

Anakin Skywalker grew up a slave on the desert planet Tatooine. His mother Shmi could not explain how Anakin came to be born—he had no father.

Anakin was a gentle child and he loved his mother very much. From a young age he was skilled at making and fixing mechanical things. When he was nine years old he built a droid named C-3PO to help his mother. However, Anakin was impulsive and liked to take risks.

Slave owner
Anakin and Shmi were owned by a junk dealer named Watto and had to do whatever he told them. Watto made them work very hard.

A Special Calling

When Jedi Qui-Gon Jinn and Obi-Wan Kenobi landed on Tatooine to repair their damaged ship, they met Anakin Skywalker. Qui-Gon realized the young slave had the potential to be a great Jedi.

Qui-Gon checked Anakin's blood to see if he had Force powers. He certainly did!

When Anakin offered to enter a dangerous Podrace, Qui-Gon seized the opportunity to win the parts he needed for his ship and Anakin's freedom. The Jedi was sure that Anakin's Force powers would help him to win the race. He was right. Freed from slavery, Anakin was able to leave Tatooine with the Jedi, but first he had to say goodbye to his mother.

Anakin was happy to be embarking on a new adventure, but he missed his mother very much.

A New Life Begins

After leaving Tatooine, Qui-Gon asked the Jedi Council to let Anakin become his apprentice, but it refused. The Council thought that Anakin was already too old, and some wise members also sensed danger in Anakin's future.

So, when Qui-Gon and Obi-Wan went on a special mission, Anakin went too.

Padmé Amidala
Queen Padmé Amidala of Naboo was only a few years older than Anakin and the young boy developed strong feelings for her.

Anakin and the Jedi liberated the planet Naboo from the Trade Federation invasion. When Anakin piloted a starfighter and destroyed the Trade Federation's Droid Control Ship, the Jedi Council changed its mind. Although Qui-Gon had been killed by a Sith, Obi-Wan promised to train Anakin instead.

Jedi Training

Anakin Skywalker returned to the Jedi Temple on the capital planet Coruscant to begin his training. He was taught how to use and control his incredible Force powers. Anakin was also instructed in the ways of the Jedi Knights. Jedi must be calm and not governed by emotions. They are peace-loving and use their skills only to defend, never to attack.

As Jedi Master Obi-Wan Kenobi's Padawan learner or apprentice, Anakin came to view Obi-Wan as the closest thing he had to a father figure.

The Force
The energy known as the Force is everywhere. Jedi learn to use the light side of the Force for good, while their enemies, the Sith, use the dark side for greed and power.

Increasing Frustration

Anakin loved and respected Obi-Wan, but often felt frustrated by him. Anakin was confident in his Jedi abilities, and felt that Obi-Wan was holding him back. He was tired of being just a Padawan.

Obi-Wan knew that Anakin had the potential to be a powerful Jedi Knight.

But he also believed that Anakin had not
yet mastered his emotions, as a Jedi
should. Obi-Wan was proved right when
Anakin was reunited with Padmé
Amidala after ten years. The feelings
that Anakin had felt for her as a boy had
not gone away. Soon he would no longer
be able to control them.

Powerful Friend

The galaxy was formed as a Republic, which meant that it was ruled by a Senate in which all the planets had representatives. As his frustration grew, Anakin found himself turning to Chancellor Palpatine, leader of the Republic. Palpatine seemed to understand exactly how Anakin felt. He was a good listener. Anakin believed that Palpatine was on his side, unlike Obi-Wan.

Sith Lord
Palpatine was secretly a Sith Lord, Darth Sidious. He served as Supreme Chancellor of the Republic—but he had plans to destroy it.

Anakin did not realize that Palpatine was secretly trying to destroy the Republic and seize power for himself.

Unstoppable Feelings

Palpatine's sinister influence increased Anakin's frustration with Obi-Wan and the Jedi Order and left him feeling very confused. When he was chosen to escort Padmé back to Naboo, he finally lost the battle to control his feelings for her.

Padmé was now a Senator and had a
duty to the Republic, but she too could
not prevent herself from falling in love
with Anakin. They were secretly married
on Naboo. Jedi were not supposed to get
emotionally attached to others. Anakin
had broken the rules, but he didn't care.

Turning to the Dark Side

Anakin had not forgotten his mother Shmi, whom he had left on Tatooine. He began to have terrible nightmares about her, so he went to find her.

Out of Control
As he knelt by Shmi's grave, Anakin was angry that he could not save her. He had ignored the Jedi teachings and given into his anger.

Anakin went back to Tatooine. There he discovered that Shmi had married a farmer named Cliegg Lars, who had freed her from slavery. Anakin also learned that his mother had been kidnapped by Sand People. He went in search of her but he was too late and she died in his arms. Overcome with grief and anger, Anakin took revenge on the Sand People.

Jedi Hero

Although he was increasingly ruled by his emotions, Anakin had not yet fully turned to the dark side. When the Republic was forced into the Clone Wars, Anakin fought bravely with the Jedi.

The Clone Wars lasted for many years and Anakin and Obi-Wan became famous heroes. Anakin felt truly alive in the heat of the battle and his powers became even stronger.

However, Anakin still felt that he was being held back by the Jedi and that only Palpatine was encouraging his talents. Anakin felt that maybe the Jedi teachings were not right and that greater power lay elsewhere.

The Shadow of Death
Padmé became pregnant and Anakin began to have nightmares about her death. He had been unable to save his mother, so he was determined to save Padmé.

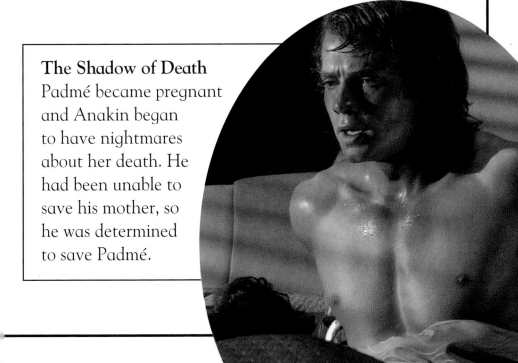

The Dark Side Wins

Towards the end of the Clone Wars, Palpatine was kidnapped. Anakin and Obi-Wan went to his aid, but it was a trap. Sith Lord Count Dooku was waiting for them. He knocked out Obi-Wan and began to fight Anakin. Palpatine urged Anakin to kill Dooku and Anakin gave in.

A short time later Anakin chose Palpatine over the Jedi and his transition to the dark side was complete. He knelt before Palpatine—his new Sith Master.

On Palpatine's orders, Anakin led an attack on the Jedi Temple.

The End of Anakin

Anakin turned his back on the Jedi and adopted the Sith name Darth Vader. On Palpatine's orders he set out to destroy his former friends and comrades. Darth Vader also became convinced that Padmé and Obi-Wan were plotting against him. He nearly killed his wife and then faced Obi-Wan in an intense lightsaber battle.

Although Darth Vader was driven by anger and the power of the dark side, Obi-Wan won the terrible fight. Vader suffered horrific injuries and burns.

Anakin the Sith
When he turned to the dark side, Anakin's eyes turned yellow like all the Sith. He could no longer hide his alliance with evil.

Rebuilding Darth Vader

Although Darth Vader's body seemed beyond repair, Palpatine refused to give up on his evil apprentice. He took Vader's body to a secret medical facility where it was rebuilt using cyber-technology. Vader needed special breathing equipment and life support systems just to stay alive.

Behind the black armor and a black helmet, it seemed that no part of the human Anakin Skywalker was left. Darth Vader had given himself completely to the ways of the dark side.

Palpatine and his clone troopers recovered Darth Vader's broken body from the volcano planet Mustafar.

Padmé's Secret

With her husband lost to the dark side, a heartbroken Padmé gave birth to twins, whom she named Luke and Leia. Loyal Jedi Master Obi-Wan Kenobi was by her side, but Padmé had no will to live without Anakin.

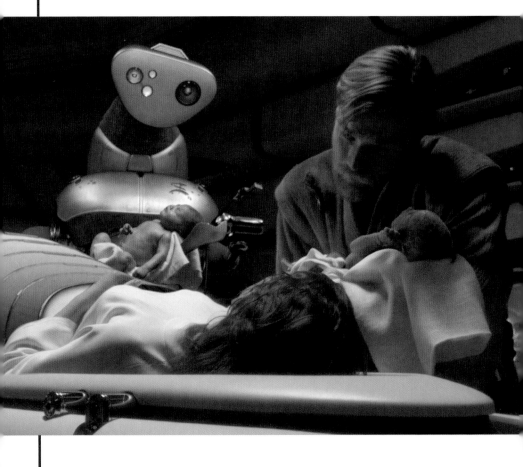

Reunited
At first Luke and Leia had no idea that they were twins, but they felt a special connection. When they discovered the truth, they were happy and not completely surprised.

Jedi Master Yoda decided to keep the children a secret from their father. Obi-Wan took Luke to Tatooine to live with Shmi Skywalker's stepson Owen Lars and his wife Beru. Luke's life on the desert planet was hard and lonely. Leia, was taken to the planet Alderaan. She was adopted by Obi-Wan's friend Bail Organa and brought up a princess. Neither twin knew that the other existed. They did not suspect that their father was the feared Sith Lord Vader.

The Rise of Darth Vader

The Republic had been destroyed and the evil Palpatine ruled the galaxy as Emperor, with Vader by his side. The Sith Lords would let nothing and no one stand in their way. Darth Vader's terrifying appearance, deep voice, and loud artificial breathing struck fear into the hearts of his enemies and allies alike. Even his own generals could not escape Vader's wrath and, as time went by, the Sith's powers grew even stronger.

Anakin Skywalker had been a brave pilot and highly skilled with a lightsaber, but the dark side of the Force continued to corrupt the mind of Darth Vader. He would strangle people without even touching them and he could read the thoughts and feelings of others.

Civil War

Although the Sith had destroyed the Republic and most of the Jedi, a small group of Rebels bravely opposed the Empire. Known as the Rebel Alliance, they were based on the planet Yavin 4. Little did Darth Vader know that two of the Rebels were his children, Luke and Leia.

The famous Jedi Master Obi-Wan Kenobi faced his former apprentice once again. This time Obi-Wan let Darth Vader win in order to show Luke that, thanks to the Force, a person's spirit continues after death.

Torture
When Darth Vader captured the Rebel Princess Leia, he tortured her to learn the Rebels' secrets. He had no idea that she was his own daughter.

Rebel Victory

The Emperor decided to build a superweapon known as a Death Star. It was the size of a small moon and had the power to blow up entire planets. However, the Rebels managed to obtain the plans for the weapon and learned that it had a fatal flaw.

One exhaust port was
unprotected and if a pilot
fired torpedoes into its shaft, a
chain reaction of explosions would destroy
the whole Death Star. The Rebels sent a
squadron of star fighters and their best
pilot, Luke Skywalker, had one chance to
destroy the Death Star. He did not miss.

Imperial Fleet

The Rebel Alliance had only a small number of ships which already bore the scars of previous battles, but the Empire had a massive fleet of starships. The largest and most powerful Imperial vessels were known as Super Star Destroyers. Powered by thirteen engines, the Super Star Destroyers were arrow shaped and loaded with deadly weapons.

Darth Vader's ship *Executor* was the most powerful Super Star Destroyer. Vader commanded the fleet, but the Emperor gave his orders via hologram.

Executor
Vader's magnificent ship led the Imperial fleet into many great battles. It was eventually destroyed by the Rebels.

Vader's Revenge

When the Rebels blew up the first Death Star, it made Darth Vader and the Emperor extremely angry. They began building a new Death Star and Darth Vader set out to find and destroy the Rebels responsible. Vader sent probe droids to every corner of the galaxy to find the Rebels' new base. He finally located them on the ice planet Hoth.

Although Darth Vader won the Battle of Hoth, he was not able to destroy the Rebels' best ship, the Millenium Falcon.

The Sith Lord traveled to Hoth with the Imperial fleet and launched a deadly attack. The Rebels had to evacuate very quickly and their forces were scattered far and wide across the galaxy.

Luke Skywalker

After having a vision in which his friends were in danger, Luke Skywalker flew to Cloud City, near the gas planet Bespin. He was now more powerful thanks to the teachings of Jedi Master Yoda.

Cloud City

Emperor Palpatine had finally told Darth Vader the truth about Luke Skywalker. As Darth Vader laid a trap for Luke on Cloud City, he was looking for more than just a troublesome Rebel—he was searching for his son.

As Luke and Vader fought with lightsabers, Luke still had no idea who lay behind Darth Vader's mask. The fight ended when Vader chopped off Luke's hand. He revealed that he was Luke's father and asked his son to join him and rule the galaxy. Despite his painful wound, Luke was strong with the Force. He refused to turn to the dark side.

Vader's Choice

For many years, Darth Vader had been loyal to Emperor Palpatine. However, meeting his son Luke—a good and true person—seemed to change him. Could it be that some part of Anakin Skywalker remained behind Vader's mask?

Palpatine had predicted that Luke would come to them and he would be turned to the dark side. When Luke surrendered, it seemed that Palpatine would be proved right. As father and son fought once more, Luke felt anger and hatred and drew close to the dark side. At the last moment Luke was able to control his feelings and refused to join the dark side. As an enraged Palpatine attacked Luke, Anakin Skywalker finally returned from the dark side to save his son.

Death of an Emperor
As Palpatine tortured Luke with deadly Force lightning, Darth Vader could not bear to watch. He picked up his Master and threw him down a bottomless reactor shaft. The Emperor was dead!

The Death of Darth Vader

At the vital moment, Darth Vader returned from his nightmare. Luke had reminded him that he was once a great Jedi named Anakin Skywalker. However, as Vader saved his son, he was fatally wounded by the Emperor.

As Anakin lay dying, he asked Luke to remove his helmet so that he could look at his son's face with his own eyes. When Anakin died, his body disappeared into the light side of the Force. Luke was sad that his father was dead but proud of him too. The light side of the Force had overcome the dark side and Anakin Skywalker had returned.

On the forest moon of Endor, Luke burned Vader's armor. All around the galaxy, everyone celebrated the end of Palpatine and his evil Empire.

Jedi Restored
After his death, Anakin took his place with the other great Jedi heroes Yoda and Obi-Wan Kenobi.

Glossary

Apprentice
A person who is learning a skill.

Dark side
The part of the Force associated with fear and hatred.

Droid
A kind of robot.

Emperor
The leader of an Empire is called an Emperor. Palpatine is the Emperor who rules the Galactic Empire.

Empire
A group of nations ruled over by one leader, who is called an Emperor.

The Force
An energy field created by all living things.

Force lightning
One of the Sith's powers which involves firing deadly electricity from their fingers.

Galaxy
A group of millions of stars and planets.

Jedi Council
The governing body of the Jedi order. The wisest Jedi, such as Yoda, sit on the Council.

Jedi Knight
A *Star Wars* warrior with special powers who defends the good of the galaxy. Anakin Skywalker, Luke Skywalker, and Ob-Wan Kenobi are all Jedi Knights.

Jedi Master
The most experienced Jedi of all.

Jedi Order
The name of a group that defends peace and justice in the galaxy.

Jedi Temple
The Jedi headquarters where the Jedi Council meets and Jedi live, train, and work.

Lightsaber
A Jedi's and Sith's weapon, made of glowing energy.

Light side
The part of the Force associated with goodness, compassion, and healing.

Missions
Special tasks or duties.

Padawan Learner
A Jedi who is learning the ways of the Force.

Rebel
Someone who opposes whoever is in power.

Republic
A nation or group of nations in which the people vote for their leaders.

Senate
The governing body of the Republic.

Senator
A member of the Senate. He or she will have been chosen (elected) by the people of his or her country.

Sith
Enemies of the Jedi who use the dark side of the Force.

Slave
A person who is owned by another person.

Starfighter
A small, fast spaceship used by Jedi and others.

Index

Alderaan 31
Amidala, Padmé 11, 15, 18, 19, 23, 26, 30
apprentice 5, 10, 11, 12, 34

Bespin 41

C-3PO 6
clone troopers 28
Clone Wars 22, 24
Cloud City 41, 42
Coruscant 12

dark side 13, 24, 25, 27, 30, 33, 43, 45, 47
Darth Sidious 17 (see Palpatine)
Darth Vader 5, 26, 27, 28, 30, 33, 34, 35, 39, 40, 41, 42, 43, 44, 45, 46 (see Anakin Skywalker)
Death Star 36, 37, 41
Dooku, Count 15, 24
droids 6, 11, 40

Emperor 5, 33, 36, 39, 40, 45, 46

Force 5, 8, 9, 12, 13, 33, 34, 43, 45, 47

galaxy 5, 16, 41, 43, 47
generals 33
Hoth 40, 41

Jedi 5, 8, 9, 11, 12, 13, 15, 19, 20, 22, 23, 25, 26, 30, 34, 41, 42, 43, 44, 46, 47
Jedi Council 10, 11
Jedi Knights 5, 12, 15
Jedi Master 34, 41
Jedi Order 18
Jedi Temple 12, 25, 43
Jinn, Qui-Gon 8, 9, 10, 11

Kenobi, Obi-Wan 8, 10, 11, 13, 15, 16, 18, 23, 24, 26, 27, 30, 31, 34, 47

Lars, Beru 31
Lars, Cliegg 21
Lars, Owen 31
Leia 31, 34, 35
lightsabre 26, 33, 43

Millenium Falcon 41
Mustafar 28

Naboo 11, 18, 19

Organa, Bail 31

Padawan 13, 15
Palapatine 5, 16, 17, 18, 23, 24, 25, 26, 28, 33, 42, 44, 45, 47 (see Darth Sidious)

planets 6, 8, 9, 10, 12, 16, 20, 21, 28, 31, 34, 36, 40, 41, 42
Podrace 9

Rebel Alliance 34, 38
Rebels 34, 35, 36, 37, 39, 40, 41, 42
Republic 16, 17, 19, 22, 33, 34

Sand People 21
Senate 16
Senator 16, 19
Shmi 6, 20, 21, 31
Sith 5, 13, 15, 17, 24, 25, 26, 27, 33, 34, 41
Skywalker, Anakin 5, 6, 8, 9, 10, 11, 12, 13, 15, 16, 17, 18, 19, 20, 21, 22, 23, 24, 25, 26, 27, 28, 30, 33, 44, 45, 46, 47 (see Darth Vader)
Skywalker, Luke 31, 34, 37, 41, 42, 43, 44, 45, 46, 47
Super Star Destroyers 38, 39

Tatooine 6, 8, 9, 10, 20, 21, 31
Trade Federation 11

Yavin 4 34
Yoda 30, 41